GARCONNIÉRE AT HOUMAS HOUSE

BEAU SÉJOUR

Watercolors of the
Louisiana Plantation Country

BEAU SÉJOUR

Watercolors of the
Louisiana Plantation Country

by

BEN EARL LOONEY

Baton Rouge

CLAITOR'S PUBLISHING DIVISION

Published and for sale by:
CLAITOR'S PUBLISHING DIVISION
3165 S. Acadian at Interstate 10
P. O. Box 239   Baton Rouge, La. 70821

TABLE OF CONTENTS

	PAGE
Foreword	vii
Acknowledgments	viii
Preface	ix
State of Louisiana Letter	xi
Eugene McCarroll House	2
Westervelt House	4
Elmwood Plantation	6
Mardi Gras	8
Temple at Avery Island	10
Houmas House	12
Garconniere at Houmas House	14
Tezcuco	16
Oak Alley	18
Fishing for Choupiques	20
Lodge House at Jefferson College	22
Nottaway	24
St. Louis Plantation	26
The Cottage (Conrad Place)	28
Ferry Boat	30
Magnolia Mound	32
Road Near Abandoned Sugar Mill	34
Parlange	36
Rosedown	38
The Cottage (St. Francisville)	40
Asphodel	42
Loyd Hall	44
Melrose	46
Yucca	48
Briarwood	50

	PAGE
Evergreen	52
Woodland	54
Sugar Cane Mill	56
Retreat at Grand Coteau	58
The Art Museum, USL	60
Beaubassin House	62
Belle Cherie	64
The Acadian House	66
The Shadows	68
Segura House	70
Frances Plantation	72
Oaklawn Manor	74
Arlington	76
Rienzi	78
Shrimp Boat in Dry Dock	80
The Beauty of the Swamp	82
Sanctuary in Louisiana	84
Crawfish	86
Camellias	88

PEN AND INK DRAWINGS

Water Hyacinths	91
Building in the French Quarter	93
Ben Looney's Studio	94
Evangeline Oak	95
Jackson Square	96
Swamp Scene	98
The Shadows	99

FOREWORD

It is appropriate that this first book to be published in full color of original paintings of the plantation homes and environment of Louisiana was written and illustrated by Ben Earl Looney, who once reported on the largest newspaper in the state, and who was the organizer and head of the first Art Department of Louisiana State University.

As a free lance artist, after leaving a teaching and reporting career in Louisiana, Looney taught and painted all over the United States.

In New York City, the center of American art, he was elected to the board of control of the Art Students' League, the leading and largest art school, which has, perhaps, produced more outstanding painters than all of the other art schools in America combined. He lived in New York City for nine years.

While teaching in New England near Boston, his students won more awards in the regional National Scholastic shows than any other students.

He still paints much of the country as a free lance artist and is as well known in many southern states as he is in Louisiana. In Raleigh, North Carolina, he has done 160 paintings; in Columbus, Georgia, two large murals and fifty paintings; in Montgomery, Alabama, 140 paintings. He represented, with three other artists, the state of North Carolina in a national show in New York while he was in charge of an art center in Greensboro, North Carolina.

His paintings are owned by ex-President Johnson, ex-Governors Shivers and Brewer, and Congressmen Caffery and Hebert of Louisiana, among many other notables. Some corporate clients include, among others: Magic Chef Stove Company, Montsano Company, Arkansas-Louisiana Gas Co., Barton Chemical Company, Morgan-Jones Textile Company, Tom Huston Peanut Company, Oconee Clay Products Company, and Ford Motor Company.

These credentials and discerning clients testify unquestionably to the artistic genius of Ben Earl Looney. It is with true pleasure that we invite you to confirm this with a *beau séjour* (beautiful journey) thru Louisiana accompanied by Ben in the following pages of some of the best of his work.

—THE PUBLISHER

ACKNOWLEDGMENTS

This writer wishes to acknowledge in particular those people who have kindly loaned these drawings at personal inconvenience from the walls of their homes and commercial establishments, plus the USL Library and Pearl Mary Segura, the LSU Library, the Louisiana State Library and Sallie Farrell and Edith Atkinson, my Agent and friend Ken McKay, the Foundation for Historical Louisiana, the staff at Claitor's Publishing Division, the Louisiana Tourist Development Commission, and a whole host of others, for assistance and encouragement in fulfillment of this life-long ambition.

Drawings appearing in this book were loaned for this purpose by the following, to all of whom I extend heartfelt gratitude: Senator and Mrs. Carl Bauer, Al Hirt, Francois Mignon and Clementine Hunter, Mr. and Mrs. Lionel Jeanmard, Mr. and Mrs. Joe Jordan, Senator and Mrs. Edward LeBreton, Louisiana State University, Mr. Kenneth McKay, Mr. and Mrs. Eugene McCarroll, Mr. and Mrs. Martin Monies, Mr. and Mrs. J. P. Owen, The Prince Murat Restoration Group, Mrs. Edward Sutter, Mr. and Mrs. George B. Thompson, Toby's Restaurant in Lafayette, Mr. and Mrs. Paul Westervelt, Miss Ola Mae Word.

—BEN EARL LOONEY

PREFACE

It has been my good fortune to have been born in a state which offers not only such a variety of subject matter for the painter, but also the opportunity for recreation when I put aside my pallette and brushes for a while. As stated on our automobile licenses, Louisiana is the sportsman's paradise. I have had the natural interest and physical stamina to engage in much hunting and fishing, sports which nature has endowed us with so lavishly. I have fished in the western Olympic Mountains and skiied on Mount Ranier, also at North Conway, New Hampshire. I have fished for trout four hundred miles north of Toronto, Canada, and hunted for the European wild boar transplanted to the Telleco Mountains in Tennessee.

But to me, there is no finer sport than waiting for sunrise in a duck blind on Pecan Island on the Louisiana Gulf Coast or landing a bass in some lake in the Atchafalaya swamp. In this same swamp, I have hunted for frogs at midnight, the many moccasins and a few alligators around adding excitement and drama to the occasion. I have a large oil painting I did of two men frog gigging with the rays from their head lamps giving an eerie spell to the scene.

As an example of the variety of life one can find in our state: on the night after I had been frog hunting in the swamp, I was in New Orleans hunting for a ticket to a performance of Van Cliburne with the New Orleans Symphony Orchestra, a ticket which I finally obtained for the sell-out performance from a lady out in front of the auditorium. The man at the door didn't want to let me in, as I still had on my hunting attire; but after I found a tie for this very important dress occasion, he relented. Next day I did a water-color on Jackson Square in the Vieux Carre.

The paintings in this book are done in transparent water-color on a full sheet (22 by 30 inches) of French, Arches, cold pressed paper.

Artists agree that this medium is the most difficult of all to work in successfully. In most other media, if the painter makes a mistake, he can wipe out, erase, or scrape off the area in which he has made a mistake, and paint it again. He can take his time, walking back to make a prolonged study. If he underpaints in oil, he may have to wait several days or weeks for the underpainting to dry before proceeding to his glazing.

In doing a transparent water-color, the artist must plan every inch of the painting before starting to paint. Often he is actually painting on water, so that the colors will blend and run to obtain certain fluid aspects, characteristic of the method. He must do this before the water and paint soak into the paper.

People frequently ask me how I can finish a water-color so quickly, and I answer that you can't do a good water-color any other way. The painting must not look "labored." It must be fluid and spontaneous. In most areas, the material presented must be suggested rather than stated fully; otherwise, if one is dealing with, for example, one of the plantation homes in this collection, the finished product will be an architectural rendering rather than a creative work of art. All architectural renderings look pretty much alike, and they have to give this appearance because they are conveying detailed information rather than portraying a creative artist's interpretation. The creative painter doesn't care if a column curves a little or the perspective is not following the mechanical rules. In fact, he may deliberately force this "abberation" for the sake of his overall design.

Once in Virginia, I quit a commission for a man who, as a professional surveyor, claimed that I drew the lawn wrong; he said he had measured it himself and that it was exactly square. I told him the only way I could make the lawn exactly square was to paint it from an airplane.

I use Windsor and Newton professional quality English paint in tubes. I usually prefer a long hair lettering brush, rather than the tapered kind. I frequently use maskoid or frisket, which means that I paint in areas I want to come out white in a rubber like fluid which when dry may be painted over and later removed, exposing the white paper. It is cheating to use white paint in transparent watercolor because white is opaque.

Most of my training was in the Art Students' League of New York, where I lived, studied and taught for nine years. However, my study of water-color was done in Eastport, Maine, in the school of George Pearse Ennis, President of the American Water-Color Society. I never saw a painting that Ennis did that I liked as a whole, but I considered him one of the best technicians in the business. I did my first year of teaching with Ennis in Florida in the new Ringling Art School in Sarasota.

Water-color is now my forte; I probably do fifty in this medium to one of any other. I do my portraits in oil.

Over a number of years I have done forty-three for the Ford Motor publications, which use water-color almost exclusively. Some of these paintings for Ford have been exhibited all over the free world in different shows. Recently, Ford gave one of them (a painting of Louisiana live oaks) to the Smithsonian Institution in Washington, D.C. At the same time the company gave others to schools in Wyoming, California and Louisiana. I have more paintings than any other artist selected from all over America in a cook book they published. The United States Information Agency borrowed two water-colors from Ford for exhibition abroad.

Although I studied water-color on the rock-ribbed coast of northern Maine, I have chosen to paint the more subtle, soft, amorphous, mysterious landscape of Louisiana.

My manner of painting may be described as realism. But not naturalism! To explain the difference to the average person who often confuses these two terms: You can paint a clenched fist in violent reds and purple and black, exaggerating the muscles, and distorting the drawing, giving a very graphic impression of realism. But naturalism means to try to compete with the camera, limning every hair, vein, shadow and exact flesh color.

I have no more patience with these artist-photographers than with the other extreme, the nonrepresentational practitioners. Their blobs of color, sans form, sans composition, sans any kind of meaning, leave me bored.

To me a work of art shows the successful communication of a valuable experience. The artist must have been moved to expend his best efforts to creating a work, and he must communicate this experience successfully. That is, if he wants to deserve the recognition of civilized people. He does not copy what he sees before him, but he must deal in symbols which have some sort of objective meaning to get his idea across. A child paints a lollypop for a tree, but it is definitely a tree to anyone who sees it.

—BEN EARL LOONEY

STATE OF LOUISIANA

Tourist Development Commission

BATON ROUGE

WILL G. MANGHAM
EXECUTIVE DIRECTOR

70804

BOX 44291 CAPITOL STATION
TELEPHONE 504-389-5981

C'est officiel!

Allons!

Passons un beau séjour en Louisiane!

Louisiana, a state of many parts and moods, has been lovingly captured and its essence distilled by a legion of writers and pictorial artists. One of the outstanding is Ben Earl Looney. A native Louisianian himself, Mr. Looney has recorded all the unique nuances of the Bayou State as only a native son can, yet has managed to provide a fresh-eye objectivity that makes his Louisiana scenes project a universal feeling. His new book is a splendid showcase of his talent and of the variety that Louisiana offers the world.

Will G. Mangham
Executive Director

BEAU SÉJOUR

Watercolors of the
Louisiana Plantation Country

EUGENE MCCARROLL HOUSE

This is not one of the very old homes in the Garden District of New Orleans; however, it is typical of the fine architecture of the old South in this beautiful section.

The classic house, with modifications in recent years, is in the center of a wide lawn, unusual in this part of the city which seems to have utilized every square foot of valuable space.

Mr. McCarroll, a retired New Orleans banker, has spent much care on the planting around the house. A handsome iron fence is at the front of the lawn.

EUGENE MCCARROLL HOUSE

Beau Séjour
Watercolors of the
Louisiana Plantation Country
—*Claitor's Publishing Div.*

WESTERVELT HOUSE

No one lives in this mansion on St. Charles Avenue in New Orleans, but in the past, it was the setting for many festivities. Owned by Mr. and Mrs. Paul Westervelt, who live in another part of the Garden District, the house will probably soon give way for the advancement of commercial interests.

Mrs. Westervelt, the granddaughter of Governor Parker of Louisiana, spent much of her young life here when her father resided in New Orleans.

This painting, begun early one morning by street light, was completed just as the first drops of a downpour fell.

Mrs. Westervelt then appeared with a friend, and we three drove to the Gulf Coast, near Biloxi, with the idea that I was to paint her parents' home. As the rain fell, I had no thought that the painting could be done, but, when we reached our destination, the rain stopped, as if on schedule.

This was just after the hurricane Betsy, which destroyed so much of the area. I have never seen such utter devastation elsewhere. The Parker house, luckily, had not been damaged, but I had to add leaves to the stripped trees.

A canopy had been erected to protect me from the rain, but was not needed. However, as I put my last stroke on the painting, the bottom fell out of the sky again, and we returned to New Orleans in the same kind of weather that saw us depart.

WESTERVELT HOUSE

Beau Séjour
Watercolors of the
Louisiana Plantation Country
—*Claitor's Publishing Div.*

ELMWOOD PLANTATION

Elmwood Plantation was constructed on the banks of the Mississippi in New Orleans in 1762 by La Freniers, who came to America from France with Iberville. This date makes it one of the oldest houses in the South.

In 1940 a fire almost destroyed the building but it was reconstructed. Thirty-two great live oaks surround the house, located just below the Huey P. Long bridge at Harahan.

W. C. Claiborne, the first governor of Louisiana, spent some time here.

It is now a restaurant, owned and operated by Joe Marcello.

ELMWOOD PLANTATION

Beau Séjour
Watercolors of the
Louisiana Plantation Country
—Claitor's Publishing Div.

MARDI GRAS

No group of paintings of the good life in Louisiana would be complete without at least one dealing with Mardi Gras.

This wild, zany, uninhibited outpouring of mirth is celebrated throughout the state, reaching the zenith in size and intensity, in New Orleans. The populace is draining the last drops from the goblets before donning the sackcloth and ashes of Lent. There are several dozen giant parades in New Orleans alone, the colorful floats winding through cheering thousands from everywhere.

On this day there are no adults; the adults have joined the children in a time of unrestrained make-believe. Whole families put on costumes and masks and they take to the streets to see what other families have done to add to the merriment. Storms of confetti fill the air; there are balloons, beer cans and bottles on the pavement (a street cleaner's nightmare).

MARDI GRAS

Beau Séjour
Watercolors of the
Louisiana Plantation Country
—Claitor's Publishing Div.

TEMPLE AT AVERY ISLAND

The creation of the late Edward Avery McIlhenny (a descendant of the original grantee to Avery Island), the Jungle Gardens are visited by many tourists each year.

Mr. McIlhenny collected plants from all over the world to form this garden, including thirty thousand azaleas, lotus and papyrus from Egypt, orange trees from Japan, and six hundred varieties of camellias.

Another accomplishment of Mr. McIlhenny was his help in preserving the beautiful Louisiana egret, the feathers of which were used to trim ladies' hats. The birds were near extinction when he sought legislation to preserve them and built bamboo structures to house their nests. Thousands of birds return here each year, along with herons and ibis.

Avery Island is noted as the home of Tabasco Sauce, produced by the McIlhenny family and sold all over the world. It has a large salt mine and there are a number of oil wells almost hidden from view in the gardens by the tropical planting.

TEMPLE AT AVERY ISLAND

Beau Séjour
Watercolors of the
Louisiana Plantation Country
—Claitor's Publishing Div.

HOUMAS HOUSE

Built on an elevated area formerly occupied by the Houmas Indians, this plantation takes its name from the tribe. It is sometimes called Burnside, the name of the Irish emigrant who came to America to make a fortune. This man, John Burnside, is said to have paid over two million dollars for the home and ten thousand acres surrounding it, which, under his direction, increased to twenty thousand. Burnside came to be known as the "Sugar Prince of Louisiana."

Five hundred slaves cultivated the cane crops, worked in the four processing mills and attended to the comfort of the owners, the prime sugar producers in America.

Houmas Plantation, at Burnside's death, was left to Oliver Bierne, whose family had befriended the young Irishman when he first arrived in this country.

William P. Miles, who married Burnside's daughter, was the next owner, and he retained possession until 1940, when Dr. George Crozat of New Orleans bought the place.

Dr. Crozat did more than any other owner to restore the house and grounds. Several of the utility buildings were not on the site originally, but their addition is in good taste and conforms to the overall plan.

The present furnishings in the house came from the Crozat family home in New Orleans. The doctor also chose pieces of early Louisiana craftsmen to augment his own collection. Included is a fine selection of early armoires.

Houmas House is now owned by Mrs. A. Genre of Port Allen, Louisiana.

HOUMAS HOUSE

Beau Séjour
Watercolors of the
Louisiana Plantation Country
—Claitor's Publishing Div.

GARCONNIÉRE AT HOUMAS HOUSE

The garconniére was used in the early plantations to house the boys of the family and of visiting friends also. Two hexagonal brick garconniéres are on each side of the mansion.

In the rear of the large garden are two pigeonniers, houses for the pigeons. Marble urns and ballustrads adorn the grounds and a number of Spanish ceramic jars are placed here.

On the day when the artist painted this water-color there were two hundred and fifty visitors in one group who had come in several busses from all over America on a tour. Other small groups continued to arrive through the day.

Houmas House is one of the best known Louisiana antebellum plantations. It was the setting of the movie "Hush, Hush, Sweet Charlotte," starring Bette Davis, Olivia DeHaviland and Joseph Cotten. Stories on the plantation have appeared in National Geographic, Life, House Beautiful, House and Garden, Ladies Home Journal and Holiday magazines.

GARCONNIÉRE AT HOUMAS HOUSE

Beau Séjour
Watercolors of the
Louisiana Plantation Country
—Claitor's Publishing Div.

TEZCUCO

Tezcuco Plantation Home was built in 1855, just preceding the Civil War, when Antebellum Greek Revival Architecture had reached the height of interior embellishment. The ceiling cornices and center rosettes in this house have marvelously executed plaster detail, and all the interior doors and window sashes still have the original false graining (called "faux bois" by the French), which was painstakingly painted by hand. The side galleries are adorned with wrought iron work in the traditional grapevine pattern.

It is a French Creole home built on the River Road in the heart of an Acadian community, and is a variation of the earlier "French Plan" house which had a central hall running through the house from front to back. In Tezcuco's plan, the central hall terminates midway through the house where massive sliding doors open into a large rectangular dining room. The front corner rooms are each twenty-five feet square with fifteen foot high ceilings, yet in its day it was referred to as a "raised cottage."

Tezcuco was the Aztec name of a village in Mexico which was built on pilings along the shores of Lake Tezcuco. Surely the connotation of a resting place built on pilings near the shore of a lake applies to this restful home built on brick pillars near the bank of a river.

The present owners are Dr. and Mrs. Robert Hollingsworth Potts, Jr.

Tezcuco is listed among the famous landmarks of the state, and its history and furnishings have been subjects of articles in national magazines. Surely few homes have been so completely furnished to the smallest detail, more lived in, or more thoroughly enjoyed by its owners and their friends, than Tezcuco. People who have enjoyed its warmth and hospitality never forget it.

TEZCUCO

Beau Séjour
Watercolors of the
Louisiana Plantation Country
—*Claitor's Publishing Div.*

OAK ALLEY

Although the house is one of Louisiana's finest, the long avenue of live oaks leading up to the structure seems to create the most lasting impression of Oak Alley.

Originally called "Bon Sejour" (Good Rest), the house was built on the site where an early French settler had planted the trees, possibly for a primitive dwelling.

Jacques Telephere Romanll engaged the New Orleans architect, George Swaney, to build the home on land acquired by his grandfather in 1830.

The bricks are homemade and the cypress was hand hewn. The wrought iron was also made here. The mantles are imported.

Twenty-eight live oaks in a double row lead from the levee to the house; twenty-eight Doric columns are around the house, and there were twenty-eight slave houses in the rear.

A two-story gallery surrounds the house. There are a balustraded belvedere and dormered windows on the roof. The fanlights above the doors are of exquisite design.

After the Civil War, the Romans departed, and later, a Sobrial family lived here for some time.

For many years this place also was deserted and, on several occasions, it was on fire. Luckily the fires were extinguished.

In 1925 Oak Alley was purchased and restored by Mr. and Mrs. Andrew Stewart of New Orleans.

OAK ALLEY

Beau Séjour
Watercolors of the
Louisiana Plantation Country
—*Claitor's Publishing Div.*

FISHING FOR CHOUPIQUES

Fishing in the bayous of Southwest Louisiana is one of the pastimes which makes the state "the sportsmen's paradise." Only the fishermen know the incomparable pleasure of drifting among the strange, wild cypress groves in the bayous while the mosquito hawks hum overhead and the choupiques bite.

This painting of a familiar Louisiana water scene is owned by Mr. and Mrs. J. P. Owen of Lafayette. Among the many paintings they have collected, it is one of the few contemporary ones which hangs in their magnificent home.

The Owens are the donors of the seven million dollar J. P. Owen Art Center at Southern Methodist University in Dallas, Texas. Mr. Owen was the second student to enroll at the university.

FISHING FOR CHOUPIQUES

Beau Séjour
Watercolors of the
Louisiana Plantation Country
—*Claitor's Publishing Div.*

LODGE HOUSE AT JEFFERSON COLLEGE

Convent, Louisiana. Now Manresa Retreat

In the flourishing days of the great plantations, parents who came to visit their sons in Jefferson College stayed overnight in this lodge house. When I painted this water-color a wall ran alongside the house and a fine avenue of giant live oaks were on the opposite side. Time and storms have ruined both.

This place is of sentimental importance to me. I spent a Christmas here when the occupants were the Brignac family, who were the caretakers during the period when Jefferson College was changing to a Catholic retreat. It was the scene also of a very festive occasion when I gave a dinner there for Thomas Benton. Benton taught in the Art Students' League of New York, where I had studied, and he spoke at L.S.U. where I, as Head of the Art Department, introduced him.

After his talk, he and the president of the university with his wife, and several other members of the faculty, came with me to Convent. In the entrance hall a long table had been covered with a red checkered cloth. In the center of the table was a large brass bowl filled with magnificent flaming red camellias, which a priest nearby had broken from the bush with long stems. We were served roast little pig with an apple in his mouth, militon, and various vegetables, washed down with some sparkling burgundy I had brought, and ended with a benediction of cafe brulot. One of the local cigar makers had especially prepared some cigars of perique tobacco, which is grown only here.

Obviously, Benton enjoyed the occasion. After the dinner he came to my home in Baton Rouge, and while waiting for his train to leave, we studied some Rubens and Titian reproductions, making an analysis of each composition.

LODGE HOUSE AT JEFFERSON COLLEGE
Convent, Louisiana. Now Manresa Retreat

NOTTAWAY

Nottaway, south of Plaquemine, was the home built for John Hampden Randolph, who owned four plantations, a total of seven thousand acres.

This house, planned by Henry Howard of New Orleans, a contemporary and rival of the noted architect, James Gallier, was finished in 1858, just preceding the Civil War,—late in comparison with other notable plantation homes.

Different in style from most mansions of the area, the columns are square, in unusual groupings, surmounted by an ornate entablature. Much use has been made of iron grille work on both the bannisters and over the large, tall windows. Intricate medallions and hand-painted doorknobs are employed inside, along with marble mantles and tiled floors. A ballroom ran the length of the house and the great room was painted white. There are fifty rooms, six stairways, and twelve black or white marble mantlepieces. In the rear is a large two story brick building once used as slave quarters.

The home, now owned by Captain S. E. Owens and his wife, is rapidly showing the ravages of time. Little effort is being made to restore or even maintain it. The home is not open to the public.

NOTTAWAY

Beau Séjour
Watercolors of the
Louisiana Plantation Country
—Claitor's Publishing Div.

ST. LOUIS PLANTATION

This home, which has been in the possession of the Gay family ever since it was built by slave labor in 1858, is located two miles south of Plaquemine on the River Road.

E. J. Gay, a merchant from St. Louis, built the house with the help of a Scotch contractor by the name of Richards, using cypress lumber and bricks made on the place. There is no record of any architect who was associated with the mansion, but it is evident than an attempt was made to show sympathy with the urban homes of the New Orleans Garden District. This was a more sophisticated style which was different from the traditional plantation of the period. In this way it was similar to Belle Grove, the magnificent seventy-five room mansion eight miles down the river (which no longer exists).

In spite of the extravagant patterns inside, which stressed the romanticism of the period, the exterior gives an impression of restrained simplicity. The roof, which is hipped, is scarcely seen because of the wide parapet of classic revival style which surrounds it on all sides, giving the building the appearance of having a flat roof. The Captain's Walk, or belvedere, is just visible over the roof line. This feature, a part of several Louisiana homes of the period, was built to give the owner a view of the ships on the river.

There is a gallery on the front, supported by six Ionic columns, the roof being supported by Corinthian columns.

One unusual feature of the home is a cellar, which, in the damp lowlands of Louisiana, collects moisture. This cellar is halfway below grade and has gutters to allow for drainage.

In the house there are four Italian marble mantles purchased from Philadelphia and a giant eleven feet by seven feet gold leaf mirror, transported from Rosedale, Louisiana, to St. Louis plantation by an eight mule wagon.

The gardens were planned in the Victorian style with a central path leading to a circle in the center. Cross sections divide the main garden into four parts.

Edward James Gay, grandson of the original owner, was a member of the Louisiana House of Representatives and later was elected United States Senator. At his death the management of the plantation was taken over by his son, Andrew Price. His daughter is the wife of Senator Edward LeBreton of the Garden District in New Orleans and they own the painting reproduced here. The artist has also done a painting of the Andrew Price Gay home, near St. Louis Plantation, for the family.

ST. LOUIS PLANTATION

Beau Séjour
Watercolors of the
Louisiana Plantation Country
—Claitor's Publishing Div.

THE COTTAGE (CONRAD PLACE)

On the day when I went down the River Road south of Baton Rouge, looking for the ruins of The Cottage, the road was muddy and the sky was threatened by rain. I had been told that there was nothing left of this once grand plantation home, so that I was pleasantly surprised to see the melancholy spectacle of ruined walls, great crumbling columns and matted vines, all good subjects for depicting tragedy,—the loss of one of the treasures of our state.

I had been a friend of Jimmy Bailey at L.S.U., who had lived here. I had lost touch with him but knew that his widow was Mrs. Edward Sutter of Franklin.

Jimmy's son met me when I drove in to ask permission to paint, and he did not have to tell me who he was. Although he wore a beard and much hair, his eyes were those of his father. He very kindly took me over the ruins and told me he would notify the caretakers I was there. He said that thoughtless visitors often came to the place, including two who came with shovels and dug a deep hole near the base of a fireplace, looking for rumored buried treasures!

The Cottage is one of two famous antebellum plantation homes, the other (included in this book) in St. Francisville.

It was built in 1825 by Colonel Abner Duncan. At the marriage of his daughter he gave the home to her and her husband, Federick Daniel Conrad. The Duncans were relatives of George and Martha Washington. During the Civil War, the house was used as a hospital.

Mrs. Sutter, a descendant of the Duncans, restored the house a few years before it was burned.

THE COTTAGE (CONRAD PLACE)

Beau Séjour
Watercolors of the
Louisiana Plantation Country
—Claitor's Publishing Div.

FERRY BOAT

It would be easy to imagine the chaos that would prevail if all traffic entering Baton Rouge today from the west had to be transported over the Mississippi River on one small ferry boat, limited in space to a score or so automobiles.

There are some of us who do not have to depend on our imaginations to recall the time the three great bridges, which span the river only a few miles apart in this vicinity, were not there.

Today, the driver of a vehicle races across these bridges, hardly conscious that they are there. He may look out from one of the three lanes of traffic to give a hurried glance at a ship beneath, but, by the time he turns his head, he is across the water.

There was a time when you got in line at the edge of the river in Port Allen, and, if only one of the two ferries was operating, you sat there, watching the boat, (which you just missed) pull out, with a few steam toots, and slowly drift to the other side. If two boats were in use, you could see a cloud of steam appear on the other side, as that ferry left at the same time the one on the opposite side did.

You had plenty of time on the ferry to get out and visit with friends who might be there, or to make new ones as you inquired about conditions of dirt roads you might be planning to traverse. You engaged in this leisurely conversation over a Coke and boiled egg or sandwich at the lunch counter upstairs.

This water-color was painted on the Baton Rouge side just before the last ferry made the trip. The dust and gravel were flying as the cars passed. An old Negro man who dressed in a flowing white costume, holding a long walking stick, had left his little shanty nearby to come over and watch. He invoked the blessing of God on my venture, as I painted.

The painting was given to L.S.U. in Eunice by Senator Frank Diesi of Opelousas as a memorial to his grandson. The senator owns eight other water-colors of mine.

30

FERRY BOAT

Beau Séjour
Watercolors of the
Louisiana Plantation Country
—Claitor's Publishing Div.

MAGNOLIA MOUND

Belated efforts are being made to restore a very important early Louisiana mansion, Magnolia Mound, in Baton Rouge.

This home, sometimes called the "Prince Murat Home," was built on a very dramatic site, an elevated bluff above Nicholson Drive which leads from downtown Baton Rouge to Louisiana State University. Great live oaks surround the house.

It is thought that John Joyce of Mobile, Alabama, was the contractor for the home. The overall dimensions are sixty by eighty feet, including the porches. Originally an early Louisiana raised colonial cottage, the house had three rooms to which later were added a dining room and two small service rooms. It dates to the 1790s. Heavy cypress and slave made bricks along with the moss and mud mixture called "bousillage" were employed in construction of the building.

There are eight acres in the present plot.

When the property of Magnolia Mound was rezoned, the structure was rescued at the last moment by the Baton Rouge Recreation Department which took custody and held it so that the Foundation for Historical Louisiana could make plans and seek help for the restoration.

Many important persons in the early history of Louisiana were entertained in the house, including the Marquis de Lafayette of American Revolutionary War fame.

The name "Prince Murat" comes from the fact that Prince Achille Murat, son of Charles Louis Napoleon Achille Murat, nephew of Bonaparte and Crown Prince of Naples, purchased some land in Baton Rouge belonging to Armand Allard Duplantier upon his arrival in New Orleans and Magnolia Mound was built on this land.

MAGNOLIA MOUND

Beau Séjour
Watercolors of the
Louisiana Plantation Country
—Claitor's Publishing Div.

ROAD NEAR ABANDONED SUGAR MILL

This squalid but picturesque road leads to an abandoned sugar mill, called "Catherine," located a few miles from the river across from Baton Rouge.

Many of the workers' homes here are vacant, some have rotted from lack of care. The hangers-on who continue to live on this street eke out an existence doing jobs in the vicinity.

This happened to me here:

They must have seen my blue umbrella far down the road, for the loud prattle that usually heralds the approach of children was not with them. The tiptoes of their bare feet made no sound as they approached, so that I was not aware of their presence until I looked up, and there they were, like two wood creatures. They stood in awe of me and the water-color I was painting.

I was at a point where this tricky medium demanded my full attention; you don't stop in the middle of a sky.

The sky, having been completed, successfully (I thought), I looked up again and smiled. The boy, about eight, and his sister, about seven, acknowledged the smile by assuming "at ease."

"That's pretty!" the boy said.

"Thank you."

"Are you a artist?" the little girl asked, lifting the wonder of her wide blue eyes from the painting to me.

"Well, I've been called that."

"A real artist?"

"More or less."

Seeing that I was a real person, she came closer, touching the edge of my panel. I cast a quick glance of disapproval at her hand, and the boy drew her back.

"I don't mind you watching. But, if you touch me, I'll scream!"

They both giggled at that.

They whispered something behind their hands.

"Are you painting that mill?"

I thought I had conveyed the idea much more ably than that.

"Yes."

"Why don't you paint it blue?"

"I guess I just didn't feel in my blue mood today. What are your names?"

"I am John, and this is Evelyn. What's your name?" he asked.

"Michaelangelo; but you can call me Mike for short. Have you ever heard of me?"

"I believe I have."

"I have," said Evelyn. "You must be real famous."

"Well, I don't like to brag, but. . . ."

"Would you give me your autograph?"

"Gladly, my boy."

I tore a page from my sketchbook and signed Michaelangelo, with an Italian flourish.

They both studied the signature intently, then John pulled Evelyn away. "Come on; let's go show mama!"

I had almost finished my painting when they returned.

"Hi," I said.

Neither answered; their expressions of admiration had changed to chagrin.

"My mama says you are not Michaelangelo!" the boy snorted.

Evelyn said, "I don't even think you are a real artist!"

The next day, as I painted near this same spot, I heard them approach. I heard Evelyn suggest that they come by, but John wasn't interested. "Let's go down and throw rocks into the pond," he said.

ROAD NEAR ABANDONED SUGAR MILL

Beau Séjour
Watercolors of the
Louisiana Plantation Country
—Claitor's Publishing Div.

PARLANGE

Parlange, on False River, near New Roads, was finished in 1750. The original owner, Marquis Vincent de Tenant, an indigo planter, built on a land grant from the French crown.

Eight generations of the Parlange family have lived here and it is now in the possession of Mr. and Mrs. Walter Parlange.

The house is typical of the early Louisiana colonial homes, using a method of construction called "bousillage," which employs a mixture of mud and moss between beams of cypress. The lower floor is of bricks to withstand the dampness of a wet, semitropical climate, the upper using the bousillage. A wide gallery surrounds the house.

Much of the fine original furnishing remains including portraits, china, silverware, chairs and beds.

Two pigeonniers are on the lawn.

PARLANGE

Beau Séjour
Watercolors of the
Louisiana Plantation Country
—*Claitor's Publishing Div.*

ROSEDOWN

Rosedown was built in 1835, but a number of additions were made later including two small wings, a back wing of bedrooms, an ornamental gateway and an office building.

The original owner, Daniel Turnbull, chose the site in the hills near St. Francisville. The architectural style is similar to many other white columned classical plantation homes. The house was furnished with treasures from Europe. Marble statues, selected by the Turnbulls in Italy, are placed in the gardens which are a striking part of the place.

In 1957 Rosedown was purchased from descendants of the Turnbulls by Mr. and Mrs. Milton Underwood of Houston, Texas, who have restored it and opened it to the public as a museum of the old South.

ROSEDOWN

Beau Séjour
Watercolors of the
Louisiana Plantation Country
—Claitor's Publishing Div.

THE COTTAGE, ST. FRANCISVILLE

When Judge Thomas Butler purchased the land in 1811, the original low Spanish structure was kept and added to.

There are twelve slender colonnettes to support the roof over a very wide gallery. There are four dormers on the roof. This long, rambling building, with so many windows and doors and the small colonnettes, together with the light yellow color of the walls, makes The Cottage unique among the plantation homes.

The place was owned by the Butler family until it was sold in 1951.

There are twenty rooms, some still containing the original furnishings.

At the rear the outside wooden kitchen and a wing, added to the original house, are still standing.

The Cottage is reached by a short drive from the highway through a wooded road. Visitors may spend the night here, sleeping in four poster beds and having a sumptuous breakfast at a rosewood table, served by maids, dressed in the old plantation styles and wearing colorful kerchiefs on their heads.

The present owners are Mr. and Mrs. J. E. Brown of Chicago.

THE COTTAGE, ST. FRANCISVILLE

Beau Séjour
Watercolors of the
Louisiana Plantation Country
—*Claitor's Publishing Div.*

ASPHODEL

Benjamin Kendrick built Asphodel, completed in 1833, a mile from the old town of Clinton.

Smaller than most of the great plantation homes of the period, it is still considered an architectural gem in Louisiana.

Kendrick died soon after the completion of the house and it was left to his daughter, Mrs. David Fluker. Sometimes Asphodel was referred to as the "Fluker House."

The next owners, the Smith Sisters, lived here for thirty-five years. After the death of Kate and Sara, the house was not occupied until it was purchased by John Fetzer.

The next owners were Mr. and Mrs. Robert E. Couhig.

Because the trees, vines and azaleas have grown so profusely, it is not possible to see all of the beauty of the building. The front with its six gleaming white Doric columns and the dormers on the high roof are seen over the lush, flaming flowers.

An unusually attractive dining facility, gift shop and overnight accommodations are welcome features for visitors.

ASPHODEL

Beau Séjour
Watercolors of the
Louisiana Plantation Country
—*Claitor's Publishing Div.*

LOYD HALL

Although Loyd Hall is in a very fine state of preservation, the exterior has suffered from additions which completely ruin the architectural unity of this beautiful structure. The rear galleries have been boxed in, and, in the front statues of questionable aesthetic value have been placed on each side of the steps. The planting and grounds have lost whatever charm they may have possessed and several garish new houses have been constructed close to the main building.

Inside, however, the original cornices, center medallions, woodwork and floors remain in their pristine beauty, the exquisite detail unmarred, although the plaster decorations on the ceiling appear as fragile as the icing on a wedding cake. The ceilings are eighteen feet high.

Because the house, near Cheneyville, was north of most of the Louisiana plantation homes we know, pine was added to the customary cypress of South Louisiana when the structure was being built. As was customary with most early homes, the bricks were made on the site.

Little information is available concerning the history of this house, but tradition tells us it was built in 1816 for one of the Lloyds of London.

LOYD HALL

Beau Séjour
Watercolors of the
Louisiana Plantation Country
—Claitor's Publishing Div.

MELROSE

Today's Negro in America, who may disdain all the fuss made over homes that once housed the bosses of his ancestors in bondage, may recall, with interest, the facts that are attached to Melrose, near Natchitoches.

Augustin Metoyer, the builder in 1833, was a free man of color.

The census of 1840 reveals that Metoyer owned more slaves (300) than any other free Negro in the United States.

It may have been true because he was a Negro, Metoyer's property was not destroyed by the northern general, Banks, when he burned so many others in this vicinity during the Civil War.

The lower floor of the house was of brick, the upper of mud and moss between cypress posts.

The two octagonal towers, shown in the painting, were added in 1915 by Mrs. Cammie Henry when she lived there.

Two other buildings of interest on the property are the "African House," a mushroom-like building with a great overhanging roof, (unique in the United States,) and the "Yucca" house constructed of moss and mud between timber.

In recent years the grounds around the house have not been cared for and much work will have to be done before the public can visit it.

The late Lyle Saxon did much of his writing on Louisiana while living here. In one of the rear houses lives a Negro artist who has gained wide recognition for her primitive genre paintings.

MELROSE

Beau Séjour
Watercolors of the
Louisiana Plantation Country
—Claitor's Publishing Div.

YUCCA

Francois Mignon, writer, and Clementine Hunter, artist, in front of "Yucca," the 1750 residence of the original grantee, Marie Therese, now a part of the group of Melrose Plantation near Natchitoches.

This house has been the residence of several distinguished personalities, and, with the African House, represents the only buildings of Congo architecture on the North American continent.

Mr. Mignon in collaboration with Ora Williams has just completed a manuscript entitled "Plantation Memo" covering many facets of life at Melrose and other related matter. The book will be published by Claitor's in late 1972.

YUCCA

Beau Séjour
Watercolors of the
Louisiana Plantation Country
—Claitor's Publishing Div.

BRIARWOOD

Briarwood, a hundred-and-twenty acre tract of virgin forest with running streams and a pond, was the home of Carolyn Dormon, Louisiana's first lady with reference to flowers, shrubs and wild life.

Her book "Flowers Native to the Deep South" is a classic referred to for the last word on her subjects not only in Louisiana but throughout the United States. Some of her other books include "Natives Preferred," "Bird Talk," and "Southern Indian Boy."

A living legend loved and revered by a host of friends for the past several decades, her untimely death this year saddened many.

She was an accomplished artist as well as author and illustrated her own books. Few could equal her skill in black and white or full color drawings of flowers.

The Briarwood Foundation under the direction of Arthur Watson of Natchitoches is continuing the maintenance of the property. Visitors are welcome.

BRIARWOOD

Beau Séjour
Watercolors of the
Louisiana Plantation Country
—*Claitor's Publishing Div.*

EVERGREEN

One of the well-restored houses in Louisiana is Evergreen, near Edgar on the Mississippi.

Built in 1830, it was the first home of Michel P. Becnel, and it remained in the hands of his descendants for sixty years. Later the house fell into a state of disrepair, as did so many of the old plantations, until it was purchased by Mrs. Matilda Gray who spared no expense in restoring both the exterior and interior to its original state.

The house, which contains ten rooms, has large Doric columns and a pedimented portico, with a double curving stairway in front. There are a belvedere and dormers on the roof.

Two large pigeonniers are on each side, and there are several lesser buildings. One, the overseer's house, predated the central house.

Along an avenue of large live oaks are original slave cabins. There are over 2,000 acres in the plantation.

EVERGREEN

Beau Séjour
Watercolors of the
Louisiana Plantation Country
—*Claitor's Publishing Div.*

WOODLAND

Woodland, sometimes called the "Payne House" and also "Macland," is now owned by the Thistlewaite family. It is situated on the road between Washington and Begs, some distance north of Bayou Courtableau and east of Bayou Boeuf.

The house was built by Dr. Louis Archibald Webb in the 1840s.

The original home of Dr. Webb stood northwest of the present structure. The first home was smaller and was located on Bayou Boeuf. At the site is now a cabin and nearby an underground cistern, attesting to the age of the place.

Dr. Webb, a prominent physician of the time, died during the Civil War. Skirmishes were fought around Woodland when General Banks came through Louisiana, burning so many of the great Louisiana plantation homes. Woodland was used as a hospital and was spared. A cannon ball is still imbedded in one of the large columns in front of the house.

At the death of Dr. Webb, the home was in the possession of the Quirk family, and some parts of the original vast plantation (four thousand acres) are still in the hands of the Quirk descendants and Webbs.

In the early 1900s the house and adjacent woodlands were purchased by the Thistlewaite family, which carried on large lumber operations.

The construction of Woodland was typical of the period. A brick lower floor supports the clapboard upper story. The large round plastered brick columns are imposing. A double stairway of curved wrought iron led from the ground level to the second-story porch. An odd and practical note was added by a carriage drive which extends through the center of the ground floor, enabling the occupants to descend from their horses and carriages without facing the elements.

Huge fireplaces warm the great dining room on the lower floor. Finely detailed woodwork and doorways add to the beauty of the home.

Many of the exquisite furnishings of Woodland are still to be seen in the homes of this vicinity, including the Stevenson house (older than Woodland) near by. Some of Dr. Webb's medical instruments are there. In the house are several products of the hand of Mallard, the great New Orleans cabinet maker of this time.

This important Louisiana landmark is rapidly going to ruin because no attempt is being made to restore it.

WOODLAND

Beau Séjour
Watercolors of the
Louisiana Plantation Country
—Claitor's Publishing Div.

SUGAR CANE MILL

Sugar cane has played a very important part in the early history of Louisiana, and it was the growing and processing of this crop which produced the fortunes which made most of the great plantations possible.

The first recorded shipment of cane was brought from Santo Domingo in 1751 to be planted on the plantation of the Jesuit fathers, (now a part of the city of New Orleans). The cane was for chewing. The early attempts to make sugar from this sweet juice were failures because the planters did not understand the process.

A small amount of sugar was produced in 1791 by a Spaniard with the name of Mendes, but it was only after 1794 that Etienne deBore (called the father of sugar manufacturing in Louisiana) showed how to produce it successfully, as a commercial venture. DeBore's plantation is now a part of Audubon Park in New Orleans. The large iron pot, used for his experiments, is now on the lawn at the L.S.U. Sugar School in Baton Rouge.

Cane production became so profitable that at one time there were 500,000 people engaged in the industry. However, the cane became infected with disease, and many people were out of work until the hybrid variety, "P.O.J." was introduced from Java. Later other improved varieties were found in India and brought to Louisiana.

Louisiana is one of the most important sources of sugar in the nation.

SUGAR CANE MILL

Beau Séjour
Watercolors of the
Louisiana Plantation Country
—Claitor's Publishing Div.

RETREAT AT GRAND COTEAU

Grand Coteau, a Catholic institution near Sunset, has provided this artist with a number of subjects for paintings.

My water-color of a statue at the end of a grove of huge pine trees, surrounded by flaming Pride of Mobile azaleas won a prize in a contest conducted by a state forestry contest, in which the painters were required to use trees as the subject.

Recently, during a reunion of the alumnae of the girls' school, a group of ladies had me do a painting of the school buildings for a prominent Mexican industrialist, whose wife attended the reunion.

I have used the magnificent avenue of oaks passing through the cemetery in composition leaving out the tombs. In one, I put a group engaged in a crawfish boil. The retreat has my water-color of this unit in the Lafayette offices.

The painting here is of the patio inside the retreat, and, to me, it is one of the most attractive views.

I have found the priests and nuns here most cooperative when I asked to do paintings. In fact, although I am not a member of the Catholic Church, I have done more work for this church than all of the rest combined, including commissions for bishops and monseigneurs in Lafayette, Rayne, Church Point, and Abbeville. My painting of the Abbeville church is on the wedding licenses and other publications.

I like to recall that at one time in history the Catholic church was almost the sole patron of the artists and I have observed that the church's love and patronage of the artists and architects and artisans has been reflected in the great monuments it has built and continues to build.

So, although I may be classed as a "heathen," when my good Catholic friends go to church, I ask them, as they leave home to "Priez poor moi."

RETREAT AT GRAND COTEAU

Beau Séjour
Watercolors of the
Louisiana Plantation Country
—Claitor's Publishing Div.

THE ART MUSEUM, U.S.L

The art Museum of U.S.L. is not an old building, but it is included here because it is a very fine example of the use of our Louisiana traditional architecture for the purposes of today.

With a little more patina of age on the walls and columns it will give the appearance of having been constructed in the beginning of the past century. It has been painted a soft pink, the color of Belle Grove and Oak Alley, and the roof is of slate with dormer windows. The fine woodwork on the panels, stairway, mantles and floors could have been taken from one of our old plantation homes.

This building is thought appropriate in Louisiana to remind us of our artistic heritage. It is true that a more modern building would have provided more hanging space for exhibitions, however there is room on the large block wide grounds for additional buildings which could be added for exhibition purposes or for studio space.

The building is between the oil center and the edge of the U.S.L. campus.

THE ART MUSEUM, U.S.L

Beau Séjour
Watercolors of the
Louisiana Plantation Country
—*Claitor's Publishing Div.*

BEAUBASSIN HOUSE

Few people, except the local natives, know of the existence of Beaubassin, because it is on a little traveled country road, one mile east of Carencro. It could easily be mistaken for another modest cottage in the neighborhood except for one feature, the stairway on the front porch leading up into the attic. This proclaims it to have been the home of one of the early Acadian settlers.

Built circa 1800 in the Beaubassin Community, an area designated on early Louisiana maps as the "Settlement of the Arceneaux Family," the house was the home of Louis Arceneaux, son of Louis Pierre Arceneaux, Acadian exile from Beaubassin, Nova Scotia, who was, according to tradition, the prototype of "Gabriel" in Longfellow's poem "Evangeline."

The house is in very good condition, even if it needs a coat of paint. The Louisiana cypress wood, called the wood eternal, is well preserved. The roof is now of corrugated metal, the material which has replaced the early hand-made cypress shingles in Louisiana. No one lives here and cattle and horses roam the premises.

Beaubassin is owned by Dean T. J. Arceneaux of Southwestern University in Lafayette.

BEAUBASSIN HOUSE

Beau Séjour
Watercolors of the
Louisiana Plantation Country
—Claitor's Publishing Div.

BELLE CHERIE

This very old plantation home near St. Martinville was built on one of the few hills in this flat land.

In front of the house are several magnificent live oak trees.

The many surrounding acres are planted in sugar cane.

The house, now deserted, is owned by Richard Chappuis of Lafayette.

BELLE CHERIE

Beau Séjour
Watercolors of the
Louisiana Plantation Country
—*Claitor's Publishing Div.*

THE ACADIAN HOUSE

Said to have been one of the homes of Louis Arceneaux, the "Gabriel" of Longfellow's poem "Evangeline," this house is typical of the early Acadian homes in Southwest Louisiana.

More than four thousand French emigrants, refugees from religious persecution in Canadian Acadia, had settled by 1788 on Bayou Lafourche and Bayou Teche.

The Acadian House is located in the 157 acre Longfellow-Evangeline State Park in St. Martinville. Some of Louisiana's largest live oaks are in this park.

The two-story house has brick walls two feet thick, lower square columns of brick, and upper walls and columns made of cypress. In the rear, the smoke house and kitchen have been reconstructed.

The house is now a museum, containing many relics of the 'Cajun past.

(The artist made two attempts to paint this house and gave up in disgust because of the frantic attention of raucous bluejays, objecting to his blue umbrella. Finally the job was completed on a Friday, on which day, the local legend says, the jays take a twig down to the devil for his fire.)

THE ACADIAN HOUSE

Beau Séjour
Watercolors of the
Louisiana Plantation Country
—Claitor's Publishing Div.

THE SHADOWS

Louisiana's best known plantation is The Shadows in New Iberia.

Now in the care of the National Trusts for Historic Preservation, The Shadows was left to this organization by the last owner, Weeks Hall, together with over $300,000 with the provision that the property be "perpetually preserved and maintained as a house and garden museum of its period."

During the last years of Mr. Hall's life, the place had come to be known as "Weeks Hall." He had employed a New Orleans architectural firm to restore the home and gardens.

Located on Bayou Teche and the main street of New Iberia, the magnificent home had been in danger of the encroachment of commercial interests, but Weeks Hall refused all offers for the property. A painter, of sorts, Mr. Hall found the maintenance of his home a labor of love.

The builder of The Shadows was David Weeks, who died before the house was completed. The lower floors were paved with brick and marble. Because the house was twenty feet above the bayou, it was possible to include a cellar, unusual in Louisiana.

There is an outside stairway in front, enclosed by lattice, and one inside. The slave-made bricks are a soft rosy pink; the roof, with dormers, is of slate, giving the house with its eight large columns a warmth that is not common to most of the white antebellum homes.

Many azaleas and camellias adorn the gardens.

THE SHADOWS

Beau Séjour
Watercolors of the
Louisiana Plantation Country
—Claitor's Publishing Div.

SEGURA HOUSE

Somewhat similar to the Acadian House in Long-fellow-Evangeline State Park in St. Martinville, the Segura home was built in 1815.

The house, on Highway 90 two miles west of New Iberia, was built on land that was once a part of a vast grant given to Francisco Segura by Charles III, King of Spain. This land stretched from Lac Tasse (now called Spanish Lake) to a lake near Delcambre.

Raphael, the son of Francisco and his wife, Senorita Maria de Prado, was born here where he died at the age of 97. Records show that he fought with Galvez against the British in the Battle of Manchac, during the American Revolution in 1779.

Married three times, Raphael gave his third wife a dowry of 250 acres.

This very old house, built of brick and cypress and white oak shingles, reached a stage of almost complete ruin, (when the opposite painting was done) until it was rebuilt by the present owners, Mr. and Mrs. Thomas C. Holleman.

SEGURA HOUSE

Beau Séjour
Watercolors of the
Louisiana Plantation Country
—*Claitor's Publishing Div.*

FRANCES PLANTATION

Frances Plantation, on beautiful Bayou Teche, was built in the early part of 1800, four miles east of Franklin on Highway 90. This gem of a plantation is perfectly preserved, and, seen through the grove of giant live oaks near the highway, it seems to have been completed only yesterday.

The original owner was Louis Demaret, whose descendants, through maternal lineage, are ancestors of the M. J. Foster family, prominent in the growing of sugar cane on vast acres today. Later the home was in the possession of Dr. Joseph Hawkins, who transferred it to a Colonel Rivers in 1876. In 1879 the property was acquired by Louis Kramer. Warren Foster bought the plantation in 1923. The present owner, Mrs. Edward Sutter, is Mr. Foster's niece.

There are upper and lower galleries on the sides of the building which face the highway and Bayou Teche. The lower part of the house is of hand-made bricks and the upper part is of Louisiana cypress. Much of the structure is held together with wooden pegs and square nails.

Two small houses to the right, as one faces the front, are of the same simple design as the plantation home and these units offer a pleasing addition to the composition which appeals to photographers and artists. A low white picket fence ties the two structures to the central motif.

Frances Plantation is now used as an antique shop, dealing with old and new decorative accessories. This painting is from the shop's collection.

FRANCES PLANTATION

Beau Séjour
Watercolors of the
Louisiana Plantation Country
—Claitor's Publishing Div.

OAKLAWN MANOR

Alexander Porter, who built Oaklawn in 1837, was an early political leader and statesman, member of the Louisiana legislature, the Louisiana Supreme Court, a United States Senator and a close friend of Henry Clay, who visited him at the Plantation in 1842.

The house, which has changed ownership several times because of war and economic upheavals, is now the property of Mr. and Mrs. George B. Thompson who have restored the place with loving care and who now live here.

Located on the Bayou Teche, near Franklin, in the midst of 250 live oaks, Oaklawn Manor was once the scene of vast sugar cane operations, employing 320 slaves.

To give an idea of the size of the building, 500 gallons of white paint were used in the last restoration.

The house is filled with treasures from early American homes and from Europe.

Oaklawn Manor is open to the public.

74

OAKLAWN MANOR

Beau Séjour
Watercolors of the
Louisiana Plantation Country
—Claitor's Publishing Div.

ARLINGTON

Arlington, on the highway east of Franklin, is the home of Senator Carl Bauer.

The house was built in the 1850s by Euphrazie Carlin, part Negro, as was the builder of Melrose, near Natchitoches. Carlin also owned slaves, at one time over 200. He was rejected by his white neighbors and was forced to sell out.

The house was on a vast plantation which ran along both sides of Bayou Teche.

The gleaming white structure today shows no evidence that at one time it was in a state of neglect and decay.

The classic portico in front is repeated on the back side, facing the bayou, and, in modified form, also is constructed on each of the other sides.

A handsome entrance gate and fine planting enhance the beauty of this restoration.

Senator Bauer had the artist do other paintings as gifts to friends in Franklin, and a painting of the old courthouse and jail, which now hangs in the entrance lobby of the large modern courthouse, which was built where the old structures once stood.

ARLINGTON

Beau Séjour
Watercolors of the
Louisiana Plantation Country
—Claitor's Publishing Div.

RIENZI

Rienzi, near Thibodaux, on Bayou Lafourche, was built at the end of the eighteenth century for Maria Louisa, Queen of Spain.

According to legend, it was built as a possible refuge for the queen, because of the unrest in Spain at that time.

Juan Ygnacio de Egana, a representative of the queen, was the first occupant, and he and his family lived here for fifty years. During this time Rienzi was visited by noted Spaniards who had come to Louisiana.

The name Rienzi is said to have come from that of the Duc de Rienzi, a friend of the Spanish Queen.

The house, now restored, and occupied by the Lavert family, is notable because of the gallery that runs around four sides and the stairway in front, curving to the second floor from either side.

The gallery is supported by brick piers. Square wooden colonettes with square capitals support the roof of the galleries.

Fine live oaks adorn the lawns and well-kept gardens.

RIENZI

SHRIMP BOAT IN DRY DOCK

This scene is "motif no. 1" in Delcambre. Every painter who comes to this little fishing village is attracted to the dry docks where the boats have been lifted up to be worked upon. This one is located so that the artist may sit on the bank on the opposite side of the canal and paint the shrimp boat with its reflection in the water. There is always something going on here to add to your painting: men scraping and painting the hull, kids fishing in the canal, other smaller boats moored close by and picnickers who come here in good weather to eat their lunches.

I have painted this subject many times, and not one painting is a copy of the other, because there is such a variety of moods and activity.

I have noticed an absence of sea birds here, especially of gulls and pelicans, and have wondered if the pollution of the water by oil companies and others is the cause. When I painted on the ocean in Florida, there were so many birds present. The pelicans would sit on the pilings and eat from my hand, and the gulls would fly down in clouds to eat from my fingers.

Attempts are being made to bring back the pelicans to our coast by importing them from Florida. This effort must receive the wholehearted support of all Louisianians because this clumsy, lovable bird is on our state seal and flag.

SHRIMP BOAT IN DRY DOCK

Beau Séjour
Watercolors of the
Louisiana Plantation Country
—Claitor's Publishing Div.

THE BEAUTY OF THE SWAMP

Those who linger in marsh and bayou discover the allure of the mists and shadows.

To those who see the swamp for the first time, it is often a wet, forbidding, impenetrable place, a habitat fit only for such amphibians as snakes, turtles and alligators.

Visitors discover that the lurking dangers are more imagined than real. The gray "funeral" Spanish moss on the trees assumes different aspects in full sunlight and under the mysterious magic of the moon. The vague and amorphous forms, seen through mists and shadows, present a lyrical beauty to all but the most insensitive.

For people who are interested in more active pursuits than the contemplation of this beauty the swamp offers several forms of sport. Take, for example, frog gigging. If you recently saw on the menu of your favorite restaurant "jambe de grenouille," or frog legs, the chances are that they came from Louisiana. Many of us have eaten this delicious delicacy, but few have had the opportunity to catch the bullfrogs in the swamp. In any month except April and May, when the season is closed, you can leave in a narrow pirogue with your Cajun guide, equipped with strong lights and snap gigs, and, in an hour or two, have a sack full of 15 to 20 pounds of jumping jacks. You are led to the frogs by their booming sounds and by the two bright spots which are their eyes reflecting the lights. Some people catch them with their hands. You are allowed to use any means which will not puncture their skin.

The swamp abounds with catfish, which are usually caught by setting trot lines, about 20 or 30 hooks strung from a line baited with some kind of meat and left overnight. One strange fish indigenous to the Louisiana swamps is the spoonbill catfish, a boneless fish (with a hard gristle for a backbone) and a spoon bill projecting in front of its mouth. The catfish are caught in nets and will sometimes strike a deep-running artificial bait.

One swamp sport which seems to be unique in Louisiana is the catching of crayfish. These are sought in January, February and March, and are fattest in the last month. A baited cage with a funnel entrance at each end is used, or flat little nets which are placed in shallow water where they can be lifted quickly. These lobster-like crustaceans are found in abundance in almost any body of water. They are free for the taking except in the rice fields and ponds where they are cultivated.

The crayfish can be cooked like shrimp and in a number of dishes peculiar to southern Louisiana French cooks.

One of the best areas to engage in these sports and enjoy the loveliness of a typical swamp is in the Atchafalaya swampland which can best be entered at Henderson, a few miles from Breaux Bridge. For a very modest fee a guide can be hired, or a boat and motor rented for six dollars per day. The out-of-state fishing license for Louisiana is five dollars for the season or two dollars for seven consecutive days.

THE BEAUTY OF THE SWAMP

Beau Séjour
Watercolors of the
Louisiana Plantation Country
—Claitor's Publishing Div.

SANCTUARY IN LOUISIANA

Toward the end of October we begin to hear them, and our faces are lifted to the sky to see these long wavering lines and swift patches of migratory wildfowl as they head for their southern homes. They really are not visitors, for they feel as much at home in their winter quarters as they do in their breeding grounds in Canada. From as far away as Alaska, the Yukon and Northwest Territory and from Baffin Island they come, converging into the Central, Pacific or Mississippi flyways, and their clear, sharp calls cause us to pull our wraps close and start thinking about some kind of southern journey of our own.

Millions of American hunters begin to unwrap their guns and put the finishing touches on their decoys and blinds. The ducks and geese run a gauntlet of these hunters' blasts until they reach the safety of the gulf marshes.

Louisiana is the goal of many of these migrators and it is for this reason (in addition to the unexcelled fishing here) that the automobile license plates bear the legend "Sportsmen's Paradise." But the state and federal governments also feel a responsibility for preserving the waterfowl for future generations, and, with sensible game laws and refuges, they are succeeding in stopping the wanton destruction of the birds that, a few years ago, threatened the extinction of all of them.

Four hundred and seventy-five thousand acres of the best waterfowl winter grounds are reserved as a sanctuary. Louisiana has the largest state owned refuges of any section of its size in North America, in addition to the federal reserves. These include the Russell Sage Refuge, 79,000 acres; State Wildlife, 13,000 acres; Rockefeller Refuge, 26,000 acres; the Paul J. Rainey Refuge, 26,000 acres; and the St. Tammany Refuge, 6,000 acres.

All were selected to give the best habitat for the intended species. There are also three federal sanctuaries of 261,000 acres. These are the Sabine waterfowl refuge in the southwest corner of the state, the Lacassine refuge in the northwest corner of Sabine Parish, and the Delta refuge near the mouth of the Mississippi.

The Louisiana gulf marshes are the winter quarters of most blue geese in North America, a big concentration of Canada geese, a few white front or Speckle Bellies, and Snows.

During a normal winter, Louisiana will winter approximately two million ducks and four hundred fifty thousand geese. The state also serves as a temporary resting place for many more fowl which fly on to South America. Louisiana is a bottle neck for this migration.

Louisiana marshes have changed little since the first birds migrated here. The food, Duck Potatoes or "Wapato," Valisnana or "Wild Celery," Millet, Pond Grass, Widgeon Grass, Banana or Water-lily, rice and Three Square Grass are still plentiful. Few people can penetrate some of the swamp land, even in the long narrow Cajun Pirogue.

One of the most interesting sights to visitors is the feeding of the wild and shy Canada geese on the grounds of the Florence Hunting Club, a few miles south of Gueydan. Any hunter knows how difficult it is to approach these fowl. At a certain time of the day they are called, and you can see them rise from the marshes and fly onto the lawn, where the men feeding them can walk among them. The guides at the club will tell you they are hard to find when you are hunting them in the swamp, and that the fact that they are fed on the club lawn does not make them easy prey out in the hunting grounds. They know when they are being protected.

SANCTUARY IN LOUISIANA

Beau Séjour
Watercolors of the
Louisiana Plantation Country
—*Claitor's Publishing Div.*

CRAWFISH

Until I was grown, although I am a native of Louisiana, I had never eaten crawfish. I knew this aquatic creature only as good fishing bait. In my part of the state you never saw enough of them at one time to make a meal, even if you were on a diet.

Then I came to the "Cajun" country in Southwest Louisiana, and, suddenly, I realized that I had not really been living before. Everywhere they were cooking crawfish etouffee, crawfish bisque, crawfish stew, crawfish pie and boiled crawfish.

The etouffee is a highly seasoned dish based on a sauce piquante and always served with rice. The rice part doesn't distinguish the concoction from any other way of cooking because everything in this section is served with rice. The bisque is made from the crawfish ground into a paste, mixed with herbs and stuffed in the upper shell of the animal. Crawfish stew and pie are self explanatory. The best way to eat crawfish is boiled. Probably this is the way most gourmets enjoy them. Aside from the delicious taste, a crawfish boil is a popular social occasion where friends get together as they do at a barbeque, dumping big gunny sacks of the live, squirming, flipping grey, green and brown crawfish into huge tanks of boiling water, seeing them change quickly into shapes of vermilion and crimson. In a few minutes they are ready, and they are drained and poured out on paper covers on the outdoor tables. Then, with French bread, lemon, any sauces you prefer, the hotter the better, and, by all means, plenty of beer, you are privileged to partake of a genuine feast.

I know a few restaurants in Texas and Mississippi that serve crawfish dishes, but I haven't been able to get them any other place.

If you like lobster or shrimp you will probably enjoy eating crawfish, which looks very much like shrimp except that the head is larger and the tail is smaller than the shrimp. The crawfish has a much more delicate flavor.

As you pull off the tail of the boiled crawfish and remove the shell, you poke your finger into the cavity left in the upper part with the head and remove a small bit of fat, which is considered a delicacy.

Crawfish are never cheap, even where they are plentiful, because of the trouble and time required to catch and prepare them. Most of the best restaurants keep a frozen supply so that they can be served through the year.

CRAWFISH

Beau Séjour
Watercolors of the
Louisiana Plantation Country
—Claitor's Publishing Div.

CAMELLIAS

We have come to associate the camellia with Louisiana plantations, because so many of the old mansions are still seen through masses of these exquisite blossoms along with the azaleas. On some of the lawns today this long lived plant has grown to the height of trees.

However the camellia is not a native of America, but were found first in western Asia. It is thought that Buddhist priests carried the plant on their journeys to Japan, China and Korea and they flourished as far back as 1200 B.C. In 1635 a hundred varieties of the camellia were illustrated on Japanese wood cuts.

Camellias were imported from Asia to Europe where, especially in France, the blossoms were very fashionable. Alexandre Dumas wrote his "La Dame aux Camellias" in 1848. In 1864 many plants were imported from France to the United States. The Southern seaports began to grow the beautiful plants which flourished in the climate.

Camellia shows are held every year in the South, where prize blooms are exhibited.

Because of the comparatively slow growth of the camellia bush, the blossoms are seldom cut with long stems. They are usually worn by ladies as a corsage or in the hair. A snow white Alba Plena camellia dusted with flecks of gold dust, is a fitting adornment for a lovely Creole brunette hairdo.

CAMELLIAS

Beau Séjour
Watercolors of the
Louisiana Plantation Country
—Claitor's Publishing Div.

PEN AND INK DRAWINGS

The technique of pen and ink is usually the antithesis of painting in watercolor; and, as a rule, the artist who excells in one of these media cannot claim superior skill in the other.

The several black and white drawings which follow are included to suggest the versatility of the artist.

—The Publisher

WATER HYACINTHS

Beau Séjour
Watercolors of the
Louisiana Plantation Country
—*Claitor's Publishing Div.*

BUILDING IN THE FRENCH QUARTER

Al Hirt, New Orleans' own famous jazz trumpeter, asked me to paint this building which he owns in the heart of the French Quarter.

The building is located across the street from Antoine's restaurant so the painter is able to ply his trade on the ancient banquette surrounded by the exotic smells of French cookery.

The narrow street is filled at all hours with visitors from many states and nations who wish to sample the specialties featured at Antoine's and admire the iron balconies and tiled courtyards of the homes and shops.

After completing the painting, I was able to follow the crowd into the gourmet's kingdom and add food for the body to material for the soul.

This drawing was one of two done for Al Hirt.

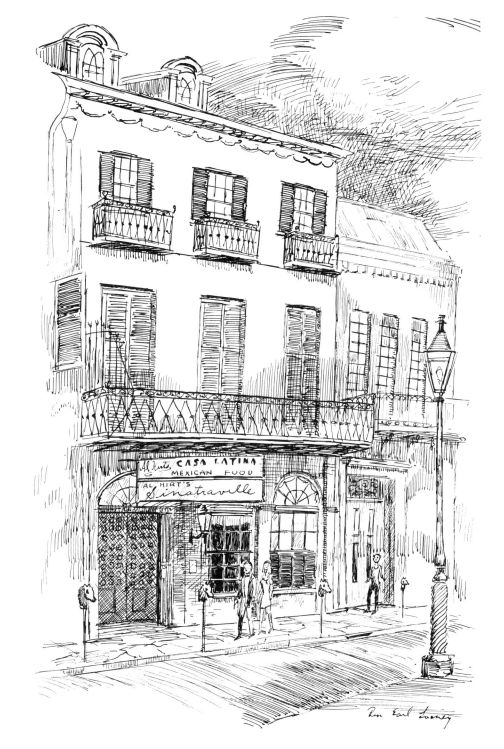

BUILDING IN THE FRENCH QUARTER

Beau Séjour
Watercolors of the
Louisiana Plantation Country
—Claitor's Publishing Div.

BEN LOONEY'S STUDIO IN LAFAYETTE

Beau Séjour
Watercolors of the
Louisiana Plantation Country
—*Claitor's Publishing Div.*

EVANGELINE OAK

Beau Séjour
Watercolors of the
Louisiana Plantation Country
—Claitor's Publishing Div.

JACKSON SQUARE, NEW ORLEANS

This is motif number 1 in New Orleans. It is in the center of the most interesting part of the Vieux Carre, the meeting place of bums, hippies, tourists and "artists." All you have to do to be classified as one of the latter is go buy a beret, some cheap art material and arrange to hang your creations on the iron fence which surrounds the square.

One of the leading art dealers in the French Quarter told me that almost any one of these sidewalk artists takes home more money every day than the gallery does. The average tourist, or rather, the average man anywhere, doesn't know a good painting from a bad one, and so prove to be very gullible when the painter is making his sales talk.

I paint often in the Quarter, but have never tried to sell anything there. In all the years during which I have known the French Quarter, I have seen only one capable man working around Jackson Square and selling his work there. He did excellent quick portraits in pastel, while his wife worked as a strip tease artist over in one of the joints on Bourbon Street.

New Orleans would be less rich with the loss of these park painters; they are an integral part of the color and glamour of America's most interesting city.

JACKSON SQUARE, NEW ORLEANS

Beau Séjour
Watercolors of the
Louisiana Plantation Country
—*Claitor's Publishing Div.*

SWAMP SCENE

Beau Séjour
Watercolors of the
Louisiana Plantation Country
—*Claitor's Publishing Div.*

THE SHADOWS (see page 68)

Beau Séjour
Watercolors of the
Louisiana Plantation Country
—Claitor's Publishing Div.

GARCONNIÉRE AT HOUMAS HOUSE